T0395140

DISASTER WARNING!

TORNADOES

by Rex Ruby

Consultant: Beth Gambro
Reading Specialist, Yorkville, Illinois

BEARPORT
PUBLISHING

Minneapolis, Minnesota

Teaching Tips

Before Reading

- Look at the cover of the book. Discuss the picture and the title.

- Ask readers to brainstorm a list of what they already know about tornadoes. What can they expect to see in the book?

- Go on a picture walk, looking through the pictures to discuss vocabulary and make predictions about the text.

During Reading

- Read for purpose. Encourage readers to think about the kinds of things that might happen during a tornado.

- Ask readers to look for the details of the book. What are the dangers of a tornado?

- If readers encounter an unknown word, ask them to look at the sounds in the word. Then, ask them to look at the rest of the page. Are there any clues to help them understand?

After Reading

- Encourage readers to pick a buddy and reread the book together.

- Ask readers to name two ways to stay safe during a tornado. Find the pages that tell about these things.

- Ask readers to write or draw something they learned about tornadoes.

Credits

Cover and title page, © Sergey Nivens/Shutterstock; 3, © Martin Haas/Shutterstock; 5, © Minerva Studio/Shutterstock; 7, © bgfoto/iStock; 8–9, © Huntstyle/Shutterstock; 11T, © Laura Hedien/Shutterstock; 11B, Capturing Adventure/Shutterstock; 12–13, © Gino Santa Maria/Shutterstock; 14–15, © Michael Derrer Fuchs/Shutterstock; 17, © Tyler Mabie/Shutterstock; 19, pressmaster/Adobe Stock; 21, © Robert Blouin/Shutterstock; 22T, © Gino Santa Maria/Shutterstock; 22M, © mdesigner125/iStock; 22B, © Jimmy Kamballur/Shutterstock; 23TL, © Wyatt Hessler/Shutterstock; 23TM, © Gino Santa Maria/Shutterstock; 23TR, © South_agency/iStock; 23BL, © SBSArtDept/iStock; 23BM, © BalazsKovacs/iStock; 23BR, © mdesigner125/iStock.

See BearportPublishing.com for our statement on Generative AI Usage.

Library of Congress Cataloging-in-Publication Data

Names: Ruby, Rex author
Title: Tornadoes / by Rex Ruby.
Description: Minneapolis, Minnesota : Bearport Publishing Company, [2026] |
  Series: Disaster warning! "Bearcub books." | Includes bibliographical
  references and index. | Audience term: juvenile
Identifiers: LCCN 2024062290 (print) | LCCN 2024062291 (ebook) | ISBN
  9798892329903 library binding | ISBN 9798895774212 paperback | ISBN
  9798895771075 ebook
Subjects: LCSH: Tornadoes--Juvenile literature
Classification: LCC QC955.2 .R83 2026 (print) | LCC QC955.2 (ebook) | DDC
  551.55/3--dc23/eng/20250211
LC record available at https://lccn.loc.gov/2024062290
LC ebook record available at https://lccn.loc.gov/2024062291

For more information, write to Bearport Publishing, 3500 American Blvd W, Suite 150, Bloomington, MN 55431.

Contents

A Windy Surprise

Strong winds start to blow.

Dirt and branches fly through the air.

Warning!

A **tornado** is coming!

Say tornado like
tor-NAY-doh

5

Tornadoes can form during **thunderstorms**.

Thunderstorms have dark clouds and lots of rain.

They also bring loud thunder.

Boom!

During a thunderstorm, the air in clouds spins.

Whoosh!

Sometimes, that air drops from the clouds to the ground.

This makes a tornado.

9

Tornadoes come in different shapes and sizes.

Some can be long and thin.

Others are very wide.

Tornadoes may **damage** homes.

They can break roads and bridges, too.

This is a **disaster**!

13

Tornadoes may throw things into the air.

The winds can even lift cars and trees.

Look out for danger!

How can you stay safe?

Listen for tornado **sirens**.

Their sound will tell you if a tornado is coming.

A tornado siren

17

If a tornado is near, find **shelter**.

The safest place is in a basement.

This keeps you away from flying objects.

During a tornado, cover your head with your arms.

Stay in your shelter until the storm is gone.

Then, it is time to clean up.

Tornado Facts

Tornadoes can last a few seconds or several hours.

These storms are also called twisters.

Tornado winds can be as loud as a passing train.

Glossary

damage to cause harm

disaster an event that causes much damage or suffering

shelter a place that keeps you safe from danger

sirens machines that make a loud sound to warn people

thunderstorms storms with thunder and lightning

tornado a powerful spinning tower of air that moves over land

Index

air 4, 8, 14
rain 6
shelter 18, 20

storm 6, 8, 20
thunder 6
wind 4, 14, 22

Read More

Marquardt, Meg.
Tornadoes (Early Natural Disasters Encyclopedias).
Minneapolis: Abdo Reference, 2025.

Peterson, Megan Cooley.
How Does a Tornado Form? (Science Questions).
Minneapolis: Bullfrog Books, 2024.

Learn More Online

1. Go to **FactSurfer.com** or scan the QR code below.
2. Enter "**Tornadoes Warning**" into the search box.
3. Click on the cover of this book to see a list of websites.

About the Author

Rex Ruby lives in Minnesota with his family. Running against the wind is one of his favorite things to do.